I0490183

VOLUME ONE

AN AFFILIATE MARKETING
BLUEPRINT

MASTERING THE ART OF AFFILIATE MARKETING

L.H.VINITH

While every effort has been made to ensure the accuracy of this book,
neither the author nor the publisher will be
held liable for any mistakes or omissions or for
any harm that may arise from using the
information it contains.

An Affiliate Marketing Blueprint

First edition.February 2023.

Copyright © 2023 by L.H.Vinith.
All rights reserved.

Written by L.H.Vinith
https://bit.ly/DvDevelopments

We appreciate that you downloaded An Affiliate Marketing Blueprint. I sincerely hope you can put this knowledge to use and start using it to start earning more money online.

Affiliate marketing has rapidly become one of the most popular ways to make money online. Whether you are just starting out or are looking to take your skills to the next level, this ebook is the perfect guide for anyone who wants to learn about affiliate marketing and achieve success.

In this comprehensive guide, you will learn everything you need to know about affiliate marketing, from the basics of how it works to advanced strategies for maximizing your earnings. We will cover key topics such as researching different programs, building a strong website, promoting affiliate products, and tracking and analyzing results, among many others.

This ebook is designed for beginners, but it is also a valuable resource for experienced affiliates looking to refine their skills and take their marketing efforts to the next level. So whether you are just starting out or are looking to improve your existing affiliate marketing strategies, this guide is an essential tool that will help you achieve your goals.

So get ready to dive into the exciting world of affiliate marketing, and start learning how to make the most of this lucrative opportunity!

Table of contents

VIII. Conclusion

A. Recap of key points

B. Final thoughts on the future of Affiliate Marketing

C. Encouragement to continue learning and growing in the field.

Introduction to Affiliate Marketing

Online income via affiliate marketing is lucrative and well-liked for both people and companies. As an affiliate marketer, you advertise goods or services provided by other businesses in exchange for a commission on each transaction made through your special affiliate link.

Affiliate marketing has the advantage of not requiring any inventory, shipping, handling, or customer support. Affiliate marketing requires more than merely promoting things and making commissions, though, in order to be successful. It calls for a thorough comprehension of your target market, a plan for successfully promoting products, and constant analysis and optimization of your efforts.
Do not be concerned if you are new to affiliate marketing. You can develop your abilities and create a flourishing affiliate marketing business with the appropriate direction. Everything you need to know about affiliate marketing will be covered in this overview, from knowing your target market to abiding by advertising laws. You'll have the resources and information need to begin using affiliate marketing to make money by the time you finish reading this tutorial.

- Affiliate marketing is a performance-based marketing strategy in which a business rewards one or more affiliates for each customer or visitor brought about by the affiliate's own marketing efforts.

- In affiliate marketing, an affiliate (also known as a publisher) promotes a merchant's products or services and earns a commission for each sale or lead that is generated as a result of their promotion. The affiliate is provided with a unique link or code to track their promotions, and the commission is paid out by the merchant when a sale is made or a lead is generated.

- Affiliate marketing allows merchants to reach a larger audience by leveraging the network and audience of affiliates, while affiliates can earn income by promoting products or services that align with their interests and expertise. It is a win-win situation for both parties, as the merchant benefits from increased sales and the affiliate benefits from commissions.

What is Affiliate Marketing?

Generating an income by recommending other people's (or company's) products.

POTENTIAL CUSTOMERS $$$

YOU

PRODUCTS $$

You have:
1. **Audience**
2. **Authority**
3. **Trust**

Advantages and benefits of Affiliate Marketing

There are many advantages and benefits of affiliate marketing for both merchants and affiliates:

For Merchants:

- ★ Increased Reach and Awareness: Affiliate marketing enables merchants to reach a larger audience and increase their brand visibility, as affiliates promote their products or services to their own network and audience.

- ★ Cost-Effective: Affiliate marketing is a cost-effective way for merchants to drive sales, as they only pay commissions for actual sales or leads generated through affiliate promotions.

- ★ Performance-Based: Merchants only pay affiliates for actual performance, so there is no risk or investment in advertising or marketing efforts that may not result in sales.

- ★ Access to a Wide Network of Affiliates: Merchants can tap into a wide network of affiliates, each with their own unique audience and skillset, to promote their products or services.

For Affiliates:

- ★ Flexibility: Affiliate marketing offers affiliates the flexibility to work from anywhere and choose products or services to promote that align with their interests and expertise.

- ★ Passive Income: Affiliates can earn passive income through affiliate marketing, as they continue to earn commissions for sales made through their unique link, even after the initial promotion has been completed.

- ★ No Inventory or Shipping: Affiliates do not need to worry about inventory or shipping, as these responsibilities are handled by the merchant.

- ★ Low Barrier to Entry: Becoming an affiliate marketer has a low barrier to entry, as there is no need for large investments or extensive technical knowledge.

★ Overall, affiliate marketing offers numerous benefits for both merchants and affiliates and is a great way for individuals and businesses to earn income online.

Understanding your target audience

Demographic information

Demographic information refers to the statistical data of a specific population, such as age, gender, income, education, and location. This information is used to understand the characteristics and behavior of a particular group of people, which can be useful in a variety of contexts, including affiliate marketing.

In affiliate marketing, understanding your target audience's demographic information can help you make informed decisions about the products or services you promote and the affiliates you partner with. For example, if you are promoting a high-end fashion line, it may be beneficial to target a demographic with a higher income and education level. On the other hand, if you are promoting a budget-friendly product, a different demographic with a lower income may be more appropriate.

By understanding your target audience's demographic information, you can ensure that your promotions reach the right people and increase the likelihood of generating sales and earning commissions. Additionally, this information can also help you tailor your promotions and messaging to better resonate with your target audience, leading to a more successful affiliate marketing campaign.

Interests and behavior are two important aspects of understanding your target audience in affiliate marketing. These two factors can give you valuable insights into what motivates and drives your audience, allowing you to tailor your promotions and messaging to better resonate with them.

Interests refer to the activities, hobbies, or topics that your target audience is passionate about or has a genuine interest in. Understanding your audience's interests can help you choose products or services to promote that align with their passions, increasing the likelihood of them making a purchase. For example, if your target audience is interested in fitness and wellness, promoting products such as fitness equipment or dietary supplements may be a good fit.

Behavior refers to the actions and habits of your target audience. Understanding your audience's behavior can give you insights into their purchasing habits and help you create promotions that resonate with them. For example, if your target audience tends to make purchases online, promoting products with a strong online presence or offering exclusive online discounts may be more effective. On the other hand, if your target audience prefers to shop in-store, promoting products with a strong brick-and-mortar presence may be a better fit.

By understanding both your target audience's interests and behavior, you can create promotions that are relevant and appealing to them, increasing the likelihood of generating sales and earning commissions.

Buying patterns and habits

Buying patterns and habits refer to the recurring actions and tendencies that your target audience displays when making purchases. Understanding your audience's buying patterns and habits can give you valuable insights into their purchasing behavior and help you tailor your promotions to better resonate with them.

Buying patterns refer to the frequency and timing of your target audience's purchases. For example, if your target audience tends to make a large purchase once a year, promoting products with a longer lifespan or offering discounts for bulk purchases may be more effective. On the other hand, if your target audience makes smaller, more frequent purchases, promoting products with a lower price point or offering regular discounts may be more appealing.

Buying habits refer to the specific ways in which your target audience makes purchases, such as online or in-store, through a specific retailer or brand, or with the use of a specific payment method. Understanding your audience's buying habits can help you create promotions that align with their preferred purchasing methods, increasing the likelihood of them making a purchase. For example, if your target audience tends to make purchases online, promoting products with a strong online presence or offering exclusive online discounts may be more effective.

By understanding your target audience's buying patterns and habits, you can create promotions that are relevant and appealing to them, increasing the likelihood of generating sales and earning commissions.

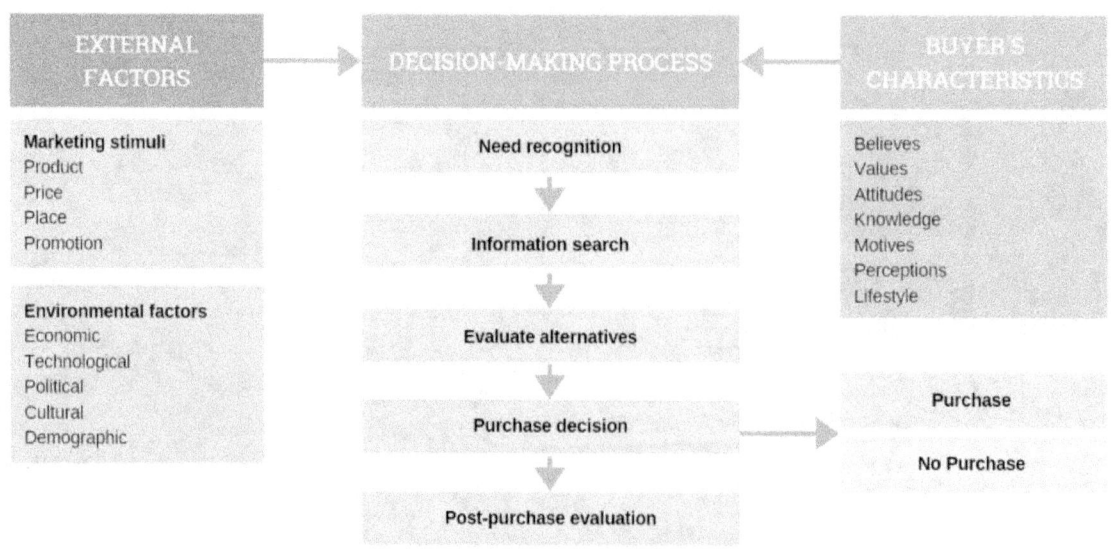

Choosing the right affiliate program

Researching different affiliate programs is an important step in successful affiliate marketing. There are many different affiliate programs available, each with its own set of terms, commission structures, and products or services being promoted. To be successful in affiliate marketing, it is important to find the right programs to partner with that align with your target audience, interests, and website niche.

When researching affiliate programs, consider the following factors:

1. Commission Structure: Look for programs with a fair and competitive commission structure, such as a high percentage of each sale or a flat fee for each referral.

2. Product or Service: Choose programs that promote products or services that align with your target audience's interests and that you believe in and can genuinely promote.

3. Reputation and Reliability: Look for programs with a strong reputation and track record of reliability, such as paying commissions on time and providing high-quality products or services.

4. Support and Resources: Look for programs that provide support and resources to help you succeed, such as marketing materials, access to customer support, and regular updates on new products or promotions.

5. By researching different affiliate programs and choosing those that align with your goals and target audience, you can increase the likelihood of success in your affiliate marketing endeavors.

Aligning your affiliate marketing efforts with your niche is an important factor in ensuring success. Your niche refers to the specific topic or area of focus of your website or blog, and aligning with your niche means promoting products or services that are relevant to your audience and that you can genuinely endorse.

By aligning with your niche, you can increase the relevance and appeal of your promotions to your target audience, making it more likely that they will make a purchase. Additionally, promoting products or services that are in line with your niche can help establish your website or blog as a trusted and authoritative source in your field, leading to increased traffic and engagement.

When considering affiliate programs to partner with, look for those that align with your niche and offer products or services that are relevant to your target audience. Additionally, it may be helpful to consider the overall aesthetic and tone of the products or services you promote, ensuring that they align with the tone and style of your website or blog.

By aligning your affiliate marketing efforts with your niche, you can establish yourself as a trusted and authoritative source in your field and increase the likelihood of success in your affiliate marketing endeavors.

Evaluating commission rates and payment structure

Evaluating commission rates and payment structure is an important aspect of choosing the right affiliate programs to partner with. Commission rate refers to the percentage of each sale or referral fee that you will receive, while payment structure refers to the specific terms and conditions of how and when you will receive your commissions.

When evaluating commission rates and payment structure, consider the following factors:

1. Commission Rate: Look for programs with a fair and competitive commission rate, such as a high percentage of each sale or a flat fee for each referral.

2. Payment Structure: Consider the specific terms and conditions of the payment structure, including the frequency and timing of commission payments, the minimum threshold for commission payments, and any fees associated with receiving payment.

3. Reputation and Reliability: Look for programs with a strong reputation and track record of reliability, such as paying commissions on time and providing high-quality products or services.

4. Support and Resources: Look for programs that provide support and resources to help you succeed, such as marketing materials, access to customer support, and regular updates on new products or promotions.

By evaluating commission rates and payment structure, you can choose affiliate programs that offer fair and competitive compensation for your efforts and that align with your goals and target audience. Additionally, partnering with programs with a strong reputation and track record of reliability can help ensure that you receive your commissions in a timely and efficient manner.

Building a strong website

Building a strong website is an important factor in the success of your affiliate marketing efforts. A strong website serves as the foundation for your promotions and helps establish your online presence and brand.

When building a strong website, consider the following factors:

1. Design and User Experience: Ensure that your website has a clean and professional design that is easy to navigate and provides a positive user experience.

2. Content: Create high-quality, relevant, and engaging content that aligns with your niche and target audience. This can include blog posts, product reviews, and other forms of content that provide value to your audience.

3. Search Engine Optimization (SEO): Optimize your website for search engines to improve its visibility and ranking, making it easier for your target audience to find you.

4. Mobile-Friendliness: Ensure that your website is optimized for viewing on mobile devices, as many people now access the internet primarily through their smartphones.

5. Speed and Performance: Ensure that your website loads quickly and performs well to provide a positive user experience and minimize bounce rates.

By building a strong website, you can establish yourself as a trusted and authoritative source in your niche, improve your visibility and reach, and increase the likelihood of success in your affiliate marketing efforts.

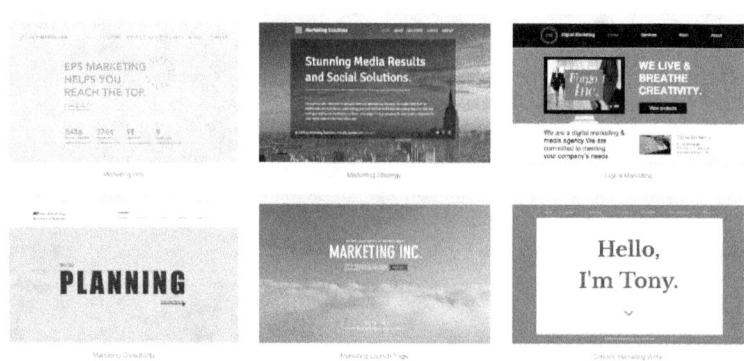

Design and layout

Design and layout play a crucial role in the overall look and feel of your website and impact the user experience for your visitors. A well-designed and optimized layout can help improve the visibility and appeal of your content, making it more likely that visitors will engage with your site and take desired actions, such as clicking on affiliate links or making purchases.

When designing and laying out your website, consider the following factors:

1. User-Centered Design: Ensure that your website is designed with your target audience in mind and provides a positive user experience. This can include a clean and intuitive navigation, clear and easy-to-read typography, and visually appealing design elements.

2. Color Scheme and Branding: Choose a color scheme and branding that aligns with your niche and target audience and helps establish your online presence and brand.

3. Layout and Arrangement: Choose a layout and arrangement that is clear, intuitive, and easy to navigate. This can include a clear and concise header and footer, well-organized sidebar, and logical arrangement of content.

4. Visual Content: Incorporate visual content, such as images and videos, to break up text-based content and make your site more engaging and visually appealing.

By designing and laying out your website with user-centered design principles, you can improve the overall look and feel of your site, increase engagement and conversions, and help establish your online presence and brand.

Content creation

Content creation is a crucial aspect of affiliate marketing, as it helps establish your online presence and position you as a trusted and authoritative source in your niche. High-quality, relevant, and engaging content can help attract and retain visitors, increase engagement and conversions, and support your affiliate marketing efforts.

When creating content for your website, consider the following factors:

1. Target Audience: Ensure that your content aligns with your target audience and their interests and needs. This can help establish your credibility and position you as a trusted and authoritative source in your niche.

2. Relevance: Create content that is relevant to your niche and target audience, such as product reviews, how-to guides, and other forms of educational content.

3. Quality: Ensure that your content is well-written, well-researched, and free of errors. High-quality content can help establish your credibility and increase the likelihood of visitors engaging with your site and taking desired actions.

4. Engagement: Incorporate elements that increase engagement and encourage visitors to interact with your site, such as call-to-actions, interactive elements, and visually appealing design elements.

5. Optimization: Optimize your content for search engines by incorporating keywords, meta descriptions, and other SEO best practices. This can help improve the visibility and ranking of your content in search results, making it easier for your target audience to find you.

By creating high-quality, relevant, and engaging content, you can establish yourself as a trusted and authoritative source in your niche, increase engagement and conversions, and support your affiliate marketing efforts.

Search engine optimization (SEO)

Search engine optimization (SEO) is the practice of optimizing your website to improve its visibility and ranking in search engine results pages (SERPs). This is important in affiliate marketing because it can help you reach your target audience and drive more traffic to your website.

When optimizing your website for search engines, consider the following factors:

1. Keyword Research: Conduct keyword research to identify the keywords and phrases that your target audience is using to search for products and services in your niche. Incorporate these keywords into your content and website structure to improve your visibility and ranking in search results.

2. On-Page Optimization: Optimize individual pages on your website for specific keywords and phrases, including the page title, meta description, and header tags.

3. Content: Create high-quality, relevant, and engaging content that aligns with your target audience and provides value. This can help improve your visibility and ranking in search results, as well as increase engagement and conversions.

4. Technical SEO: Ensure that your website is technically sound and follows best practices for SEO, such as having a sitemap, using proper URL structure, and having a responsive design.

5. Link Building: Build high-quality backlinks to your website from other reputable websites in your niche. This can help improve your visibility and ranking in search results, as well as establish your online presence and authority.

By optimizing your website for search engines, you can increase your visibility and reach, attract more qualified traffic to your site, and support your affiliate marketing efforts.

Promoting affiliate products

Promoting affiliate products is the core of affiliate marketing, as it involves promoting and recommending products to your target audience in exchange for commissions. There are several strategies that you can use to promote affiliate products effectively, including:

→ Product Reviews: Write detailed and honest product reviews that highlight the features, benefits, and drawbacks of the products you are promoting. This can help establish your credibility and position you as a trusted source of information in your niche.

→ How-To Guides: Create how-to guides or tutorials that show how to use the products you are promoting. This can help educate your target audience and increase their likelihood of making a purchase.

→ Comparison Posts: Compare different products in your niche and highlight their similarities and differences. This can help your target audience make informed buying decisions and increase their likelihood of making a purchase through your affiliate link.

→ Social Media: Utilize social media platforms to promote your affiliate products, such as sharing product reviews and how-to guides, participating in relevant conversations and groups, and leveraging influencer marketing.

→ Influencer Marketing: Partner with influencers in your niche to promote your affiliate products. Influencers have a large following and can help increase your reach and visibility, as well as drive traffic and sales to your site.

→ Email Marketing: Utilize email marketing to promote your affiliate products to your subscribers. This can help increase conversions and build a relationship with your target audience.

By effectively promoting affiliate products, you can increase conversions, drive sales, and earn commissions as an affiliate marketer.

Creating content around affiliate products is a key aspect of affiliate marketing, as it allows you to promote the products you are affiliated with and provide value to your target audience. Here are a few tips to help you create effective content around affiliate products:

1. Know Your Audience: Understanding your target audience and their needs, interests, and pain points is essential to creating content that resonates with them. This will help you create content that is relevant, useful, and engaging to your audience.

2. Choose Relevant Products: When selecting affiliate products to promote, choose those that are relevant and aligned with your niche. This will help ensure that your content is relevant to your target audience and increases the likelihood of conversions.

3. Provide Value: When creating content around affiliate products, focus on providing value to your target audience. This can include sharing your personal experience with the product, offering tips and advice, and highlighting its benefits.

4. Be Honest: Be honest and transparent in your content, and always disclose that you are an affiliate marketer. This will help build trust with your target audience and increase the likelihood of conversions.

5. Be Creative: Be creative in your content creation and explore different formats, such as blog posts, product reviews, how-to guides, and video content. This will help keep your content fresh, engaging, and appealing to your target audience.

6. Optimize for SEO: Optimize your content for search engines by incorporating relevant keywords, using meta descriptions, and including internal and external links. This will help increase the visibility and ranking of your content in search engine results pages (SERPs).

By creating valuable content around affiliate products, you can build relationships with your target audience, increase conversions, and grow your affiliate marketing business.

AFFILIATE
MARKETING
CONTENT

Utilizing social media platforms is a powerful way to promote affiliate products and reach a large audience. Here are some tips to help you effectively utilize social media for affiliate marketing:

1. Choose the Right Platforms: Choose social media platforms that are relevant to your target audience and align with your niche. For example, if you are promoting fashion products, Instagram and Pinterest may be the best platforms to use.

2. Build a Strong Presence: Build a strong presence on the social media platforms you choose by creating a professional profile, posting regular updates, and engaging with your followers.

3. Share Relevant Content: Share relevant and valuable content on your social media platforms, such as product reviews, how-to guides, and tutorials. This will help educate your followers and increase the likelihood of conversions.

4. Utilize Influencer Marketing: Partner with influencers in your niche to promote your affiliate products. Influencers have a large following and can help increase your reach and visibility, as well as drive traffic and sales to your site.

5. Leverage Hashtags: Leverage relevant hashtags to reach a wider audience and increase the visibility of your posts.

6. Engage with Your Followers: Engage with your followers by responding to their comments and messages, and participating in relevant conversations and groups. This will help build relationships with your target audience and increase the likelihood of conversions.

By effectively utilizing social media platforms, you can reach a large audience, increase conversions, and grow your affiliate marketing business.

Influencer marketing

Influencer marketing is a popular strategy used in affiliate marketing, where businesses partner with influential individuals in a particular niche to promote their products. Influencers have a large following and can help increase visibility, reach, and conversions for affiliate marketers. Here are some tips for using influencer marketing in affiliate marketing:

1. Identify Relevant Influencers: Identify influencers who are relevant to your niche and have a following that aligns with your target audience. This will help ensure that your products are promoted to the right people.

2. Establish Relationships: Establish relationships with influencers by engaging with their content, commenting on their posts, and reaching out to them directly. Building a personal connection with influencers will help increase the likelihood of a successful partnership.

3. Offer Fair Compensation: Offer fair compensation for influencer marketing partnerships, such as commission-based compensation or a flat fee. This will help ensure that influencers are motivated to promote your products effectively.

4. Provide Clear Guidelines: Provide clear guidelines for influencer marketing partnerships, including the type of content to be created, the length of the partnership, and any specific requirements. This will help ensure that both parties are on the same page and that the partnership runs smoothly.

5. Measure Success: Measure the success of your influencer marketing partnerships by tracking metrics such as traffic, sales, and conversions. This will help you understand the impact of the partnership and make informed decisions about future partnerships.

Influencer marketing can be a highly effective strategy for affiliate marketing, as it allows you to reach a large and engaged audience, increase conversions, and build your brand. However, it is important to approach influencer marketing with a strategic and thoughtful approach to ensure its success.

Tracking and analyzing results

Tracking and analyzing results is an important aspect of affiliate marketing, as it helps you understand the effectiveness of your strategies and make informed decisions about future efforts. Here are some tips for tracking and analyzing your results:

→ Set Clear Goals: Set clear and specific goals for your affiliate marketing efforts, such as increasing sales, website traffic, or conversions. This will help you measure the success of your efforts and determine if you are on track to achieve your goals.

→ Use Analytics Tools: Use analytics tools, such as Google Analytics, to track key metrics, such as website traffic, conversion rates, and sales. These tools will help you understand the performance of your website and your affiliate marketing efforts.

→ Monitor Sales and Commission: Monitor sales and commission payments to ensure that you are earning the correct amount for each sale. This will help you identify any discrepancies and resolve any issues quickly.

→ Track Your Marketing Efforts: Track your marketing efforts, including social media posts, email campaigns, and influencer marketing partnerships. This will help you understand which strategies are working best and where you should focus your efforts in the future.

→ Analyze Results: Analyze your results on a regular basis, such as weekly or monthly, to understand the impact of your efforts and identify areas for improvement. This will help you make informed decisions about future strategies and refine your approach to affiliate marketing.

By tracking and analyzing your results, you can gain a deeper understanding of your affiliate marketing efforts, identify areas for improvement, and make informed decisions about future strategies. This will help you grow your affiliate marketing business and achieve your goals.

Setting measurable goals

Setting measurable goals is a critical step in affiliate marketing, as it helps you stay focused, track your progress, and determine if you are on track to achieve your desired outcomes. Here are some tips for setting measurable goals in affiliate marketing:

1. Be Specific: Set specific, measurable, and achievable goals, such as increasing website traffic by 20% in the next six months, or earning $10,000 in commission in the next year.

2. Make Them Time-Bound: Set goals with a specific timeline, such as in the next six months or by the end of the year. This helps you stay focused and motivated, as you have a clear deadline to work towards.

3. Prioritize Goals: Prioritize your goals, focusing on the most important ones first. This will help you stay focused and avoid spreading yourself too thin.

4. Consider Your Resources: Consider your resources, such as time, budget, and manpower, when setting goals. Make sure your goals are realistic and achievable given your current resources.

5. Review and Revise: Regularly review and revise your goals to ensure that they remain relevant and achievable. This will help you stay on track and make any necessary adjustments to your strategy.

By setting measurable goals, you can stay focused and motivated, track your progress, and determine if you are on track to achieve your desired outcomes. This will help you succeed in affiliate marketing and grow your business.

Using analytics tools is a key component of affiliate marketing, as it allows you to track the performance of your website, marketing efforts, and affiliate products. Here are some tips for using analytics tools effectively:

1. Choose the Right Tools: Choose the right analytics tools for your needs, such as Google Analytics, which is a popular and powerful tool for tracking website traffic and conversions.

2. Set Up Tracking: Set up tracking for key metrics, such as website traffic, conversion rates, and sales. This will help you understand the performance of your website and your affiliate marketing efforts.

3. Track Your Marketing Efforts: Track your marketing efforts, such as social media posts, email campaigns, and influencer marketing partnerships, to understand which strategies are working best.

4. Monitor Sales and Commission: Monitor sales and commission payments to ensure that you are earning the correct amount for each sale.

5. Analyze Results: Analyze your results on a regular basis, such as weekly or monthly, to understand the impact of your efforts and identify areas for improvement.

By using analytics tools effectively, you can gain a deeper understanding of your affiliate marketing efforts, track your progress, and make informed decisions about future strategies. This will help you succeed in affiliate marketing and grow your business.

Continuously optimizing your affiliate marketing strategy is important to ensure that you are staying ahead of the competition and maximizing your earning potential. Here are some tips for continuously optimizing your strategy:

1. Stay Up-to-Date: Stay up-to-date with industry trends, changes in consumer behavior, and new technologies to ensure that your strategy remains relevant and effective.

2. Monitor Competitor Activity: Monitor your competitors' activities and strategies to understand their strengths and weaknesses, and identify opportunities to differentiate yourself and stand out from the crowd.

3. Test and Experiment: Test different strategies and tactics to determine what works best for your target audience and niche. For example, you could test different social media platforms, email campaigns, or influencer partnerships to see what generates the most sales and commissions.

4. Ask for Feedback: Ask for feedback from your target audience, customers, and affiliates to understand what they like and dislike about your strategy and identify opportunities for improvement.

5. Make Data-Driven Decisions: Make data-driven decisions, using the insights and information gained from analytics tools and feedback, to optimize your strategy and make informed decisions about future initiatives.

By continuously optimizing your affiliate marketing strategy, you can stay ahead of the competition, maximize your earning potential, and grow your business over time.

Staying compliant with advertising regulations

Staying compliant with advertising regulations is an important aspect of affiliate marketing to ensure that your business is operating legally and ethically. Here are some tips for staying compliant with advertising regulations:

→ Familiarize Yourself with the Law: Familiarize yourself with the law and regulations surrounding affiliate marketing, such as the Federal Trade Commission's guidelines for advertising and marketing.

→ Be Transparent: Be transparent about your affiliate relationships and disclose them clearly and prominently on your website and in your marketing materials.

→ Use No-Follow Links: Use no-follow links when promoting affiliate products to ensure that you are not passing on link juice and influencing search engine rankings.

→ Avoid Deceptive Practices: Avoid deceptive practices, such as misleading headlines, fake reviews, and false claims, which can result in legal consequences and harm your reputation.

→ Keep Records: Keep records of all your affiliate relationships, commission payments, and advertising expenses, as these will be required if you are audited by the government or sued by a customer.

By staying compliant with advertising regulations, you can avoid legal consequences, protect your reputation, and build trust with your target audience. This will help you succeed in affiliate marketing and grow your business.

Understanding FTC guidelines

The Federal Trade Commission (FTC) is the primary regulatory body responsible for enforcing advertising and marketing laws in the United States. To ensure that your affiliate marketing practices are compliant with FTC guidelines, it is important to understand the following key points:

1. Endorsement Guidelines: The FTC requires that all affiliate marketers disclose their relationships with merchants and clearly state that they are being paid for promoting their products. This helps consumers to make informed purchasing decisions and ensures that the marketing materials are not misleading.

2. Truth in Advertising: The FTC requires that all advertising and marketing materials be truthful and not misleading. This includes claims about the benefits, features, and results of using the affiliate products, as well as the earnings potential of the affiliate program.

3. Affiliate Disclosures: The FTC requires that all affiliate disclosures be clear and conspicuous, meaning that they must be noticeable and easily understandable to the average consumer.

4. Testimonials and Reviews: The FTC requires that testimonials and reviews be truthful and not misleading, and that they reflect the actual experiences of the people who wrote them. Affiliate marketers cannot use fake reviews or manipulate the results of surveys or testimonials to make the products appear more attractive.

By understanding FTC guidelines, you can ensure that your affiliate marketing practices are legal, ethical, and in compliance with the law. This will help you to build trust with your target audience, avoid legal consequences, and grow your business over time.

Properly disclosing affiliate relationships

Properly disclosing affiliate relationships is essential for building trust with your target audience and staying compliant with advertising regulations. Here are some tips for properly disclosing affiliate relationships:

1. Use Affiliate Disclosures: Use clear and conspicuous affiliate disclosures in all your marketing materials, including your website, social media posts, and email campaigns.

2. Be Clear and Specific: Be clear and specific about your affiliate relationships, including the fact that you are being paid for promoting the affiliate products.

3. Use No-Follow Links: Use no-follow links in your affiliate marketing to ensure that you are not passing on link juice and influencing search engine rankings.

4. Place Disclosures in a Prominent Location: Place affiliate disclosures in a prominent location, such as the top or bottom of the page, to ensure that they are easily noticed by your target audience.

5. Use the Same Language: Use the same language and format for your affiliate disclosures in all your marketing materials to ensure consistency and to make it easy for consumers to understand your relationships.

By properly disclosing your affiliate relationships, you can build trust with your target audience, avoid legal consequences, and grow your business over time. This will help you to succeed in affiliate marketing and achieve your goals.

Keeping up-to-date with industry regulations

Keeping up-to-date with industry regulations is important for ensuring that your affiliate marketing practices are compliant with the law and that you are able to grow your business over time. Here are some tips for keeping up-to-date with industry regulations:

1. Follow Industry News and Updates: Follow industry news and updates to stay informed about changes in affiliate marketing regulations, including changes to FTC guidelines, advertising laws, and consumer protection laws.

2. Subscribe to Industry Newsletters: Subscribe to industry newsletters and blogs to receive regular updates about changes in affiliate marketing regulations and best practices.

3. Attend Industry Conferences and Events: Attend industry conferences and events to learn about new trends and developments in affiliate marketing and to network with other professionals in the field.

4. Seek Legal Advice: Seek legal advice from a qualified attorney to ensure that your affiliate marketing practices are compliant with the law and that you are avoiding legal consequences.

By keeping up-to-date with industry regulations, you can ensure that your affiliate marketing practices are legal, ethical, and in compliance with the law. This will help you to build trust with your target audience, avoid legal consequences, and grow your business over time.

Conclusion

In conclusion, affiliate marketing can be a very lucrative and successful way to make money online, but it demands a lot of effort, commitment, and industry knowledge. Understanding your target market, adhering to your niche, assessing commission rates and payment structures, developing a solid website, promoting affiliate items, and continuously refining your plan are all necessary for success in affiliate marketing. Additionally, it's crucial to adhere to advertising standards and stay current on industry regulations by reading news articles, going to events, and consulting a lawyer. You can succeed in affiliate marketing by using these suggestions and always learning new things.

Recap of key points

Here's a recap of the key points discussed:
1. Understand your target audience, including their demographic information, interests and behaviors, and buying patterns and habits.

2. Research different affiliate programs and align with your niche.

3. Evaluate commission rates and payment structures.

4. Build a strong website with a good design and layout and create high-quality content.

5. Promote affiliate products by creating content around them and utilizing social media platforms, such as influencer marketing.

6. Track and analyze results by setting measurable goals and using analytics tools.

7. Continuously optimize your strategy by analyzing your results and making changes as needed.

8. Stay compliant with advertising regulations by understanding FTC guidelines and properly disclosing affiliate relationships.

9. Keep up-to-date with industry regulations by following news and updates, attending events, and seeking legal advice.

By following these key points, you can build a successful affiliate marketing business that earns you money and helps you achieve your goals.

Final thoughts on the future of Affiliate Marketing

With more companies discovering the advantages of this marketing technique and including it as a crucial component of their marketing plans, the future of affiliate marketing appears to be bright. It is expected that as technology develops, affiliate marketing will become even more sophisticated, presenting affiliates with additional chances to connect with their target audience and make money.

The rise of mobile and the rising use of mobile devices are two trends to monitor in the future of affiliate marketing. Affiliates will be able to contact their target audience while on the go thanks to programs for affiliate marketing that are anticipated to become more mobile-friendly. Additionally, it's expected that machine learning and artificial intelligence will be used more frequently in affiliate marketing, enabling affiliates to more precisely track their outcomes and more efficiently target their audience.

Another trend to watch is the rise of influencer marketing, which has already become a popular way for affiliates to reach their target audience and promote products. As influencer marketing continues to grow, affiliates are likely to be able to work with a wider range of influencers and use more sophisticated tools to track the success of their campaigns.

Overall, the future of affiliate marketing looks bright, offering numerous opportunities for growth and success. By staying up-to-date with industry trends and continuing to learn and improve, affiliates can ensure that they are well-positioned to take advantage of these opportunities and succeed in the future.

Encouragement to continue learning and growing in the field

It's important to remember that affiliate marketing is a constantly evolving field, and there is always room for growth and improvement. As technology advances and consumer behaviors change, it is essential for affiliates to stay up-to-date and continue learning about the latest trends and best practices in the industry.

To continue growing and improving in affiliate marketing, it's important to:

★ Stay informed about industry news and updates.

★ Attend events and conferences to network with other affiliates and learn from experts in the field.

★ Read books, blogs, and other resources to stay up-to-date on the latest trends and best practices.

★ Try new strategies and approaches, and don't be afraid to experiment and make mistakes.

★ Collaborate with other affiliates and seek out mentorship opportunities to learn from experienced marketers.

By continuously learning and growing, you can stay ahead of the curve in affiliate marketing and achieve greater success in the future. So don't be afraid to embrace change and keep learning, and you will be well on your way to a successful and rewarding career in affiliate marketing.

Thank You for previewing this eBook

- The image content is not a stock photo. Copyrights for images belong to their respective owners.

L.H.Vinith Presents:

AN AFFILIATE
MARKETING
BLUEPRINT

**A STEP-BY-STEP
PROCESS**

https://bit.ly/DvDevelopments

www.ingramcontent.com/pod-product-compliance
Lightning Source LLC
Chambersburg PA
CBHW082155230526
45467CB00044B/3417